ANOTHER ROUND

OF

ICE COLD BEER

My 365 More Random Thoughts To Improve Your Life Not One Iota

By

Chris Gay

Suesea Press
Manchester, Connecticut
The Passion of the Chris, LLC

Cover design by Debbie Tosun Kilday
Kilday Krafts

Interior Layout by Ryan Twomey-Allaire

ISBN 978-0-9844673-3-4

www.chrisjgay.com

Also by Chris Gay

Novels

Ghost of a Chance

Novellas

Sherlock Holmes and the Final Reveal

Humor

Something Witty this Way Comes

The Bachelor Cookbook: Edible Meals with a Side of Sarcasm

Shouldn't Ice Cold Beer Be Frozen? My 365 Random Thoughts to Improve Your Life Not One Iota

And That's the Way It Was…Give or Take: A Daily Dose of My Radio Writings

Upcoming Fiction

Perdition's Wrath

Christmas

Kringle: From Man to Myth

Dedication

This book is dedicated to a great circle of friends. I'd list them individually but that would require alphabetizing, which is just too much effort for a humor book. For my novels, sure. They're solid literature. But come on, this thing's got two frosted mugs of beer on its cover.

"Humor is mankind's greatest blessing."

-Mark Twain

"I come from a long line of generations."

-Charles M. Schulz

Introduction

So here we are again, you and me. Of course, I write that assuming you've already read this book's predecessor, *Shouldn't Ice Cold Beer be Frozen? My 365 Random Thoughts to Improve Your Life Not One Iota*. If you haven't, perhaps you should stop right here and purchase it, too. Oh, all right. Listen. (Or more accurately, read) Integrity, an unfortunate character flaw, obliges me to tell you that you really don't need to buy the former book to enjoy the contents of this latter one. The only real variance between the two is that they contain different random thoughts. (Which you might expect) This book and its forerunner are the rare exception of affiliated books in which it couldn't possibly matter less if they're read out of order. Unlike my three other humor books, *The Bachelor Cookbook: Edible Meals with a Side of Sarcasm, And That's the Way it Was...Give or Take: A Daily Dose of My Radio Writings* and *Something Witty this Way Comes*; or even my serious books, the extraordinary paranormal, theological thriller novel *Ghost of a Chance* and, with its astonishing twist, *Sherlock Holmes and the Final Reveal*, these two are simply comprised of hundreds of random, mostly humorous thoughts designed to make you laugh. Or at the very least, think. Read them in any order you wish, and try to forget how extraordinarily blatant the self-promotion of my other books was two sentences back. Look, it's not about avarice and greed; I make such references simply as a good luck gesture to myself. It's no different from christening a ship with a bottle of champagne or putting a horseshoe up in your kitchen. And if you actually believe that, all the better. Now on to the comedy. We'll meet again at the *Afterword*.

1   You can judge a book's cover by its cover.

ಬಂಧ

2   Instead of *"Get Out!"* just once I wish a movie would have a ghostly voice say something more constructive to its homeowner, like *"Easy on the oregano, Julie. You don't want to overpower the tomato sauce."*

ಬಂಧ

3   These dollar store headphones have turned out to be nothing more than cheap junk.

ಬಂಧ

4   Doesn't *Words with Adversaries* sound like it would be more fun to play?

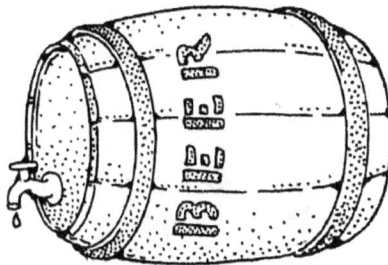

5 Just once I'd like to read about the healing properties of *Oreos*.

ஐ௸

6 When you buy fried dough it has to be with sugar and cinnamon. With sauce, all you have is a pizza for lactose intolerants.

ஐ௸

7 I'd like to pitch a show to *Discovery Channel* that features a group of timid-yet-curious meteorologists who follow around sun showers and snow flurries. I'd call it *Mediocre Storm Chasers*.

8 That *Witch of the West* seemed more incompetent than *wicked*. And really, if you know that water will destroy you why would you keep buckets of it hanging around your home? I mean even just filling them up would be risky.

ಬಂಣ

9 If a black and white cat crosses your path I wonder if it means 3.5 years of bad luck, or if it's a pro-rata calculation based upon the percentage of colors displayed by that individual feline.

ಬಂಣ

10 Even if I could believe that George Jetson's car was able to fold up into a briefcase, there's no way I would ever buy that he could lift it.

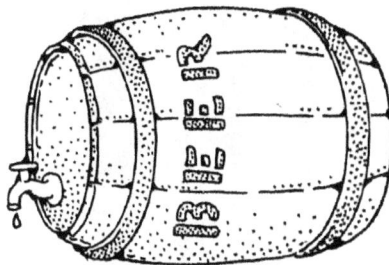

11 I wonder what they call people who don't believe in the existence of Atheism.

ଧରଔ

12 The harder you work toward achieving success, the more likely you are to leave Opportunity no choice but to knock on your door.

ଧରଔ

13 If a company can actually call its cheese *HeluvaGood*, it's probably just a matter of time before we're able to wash it down with some *PhuckenGrate* beer.

14 It's always one second after finally lying comfortably that an itch occurs in a place where you'd need the dexterity of a Flying Wallenda to reach.

ಲ೦ೞ

15 If you want to liven things up at your next dinner party, while putting out the shrimp cocktail casually suggest the possibility that both *Evolution* and *Creationism* simply co-exist.

ಲ೦ೞ

16 A broken digital clock isn't right any times a day.

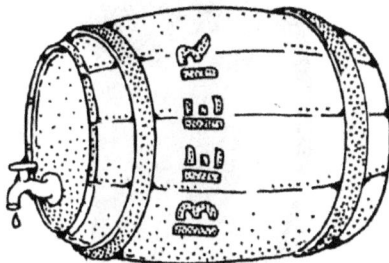

17 Though certainly refreshing, the *Diet Pepsi* I'm drinking as I write this just seems a little too tame to be labeled "wild" cherry.

ೞಅ

18 What this world needs are more websites that could tell you if your tie matched your shirt.

ೞಅ

19 When I was very young the only reason I ever considered being an astronaut was for their seemingly endless access to *Tang*.

20 Don't try to tell me that you've never pried a few batteries out of a wall clock to replace the ones that just ran out in your TV remote control.

ଽଓଔ

21 The irony of failure is that it's so easy to achieve, you can set it as a goal and be assured of success.

ଽଓଔ

22 Comic strip characters must save thousands of dollars on clothing expenses.

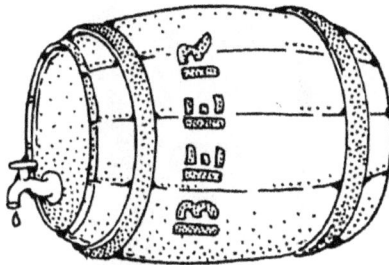

23 A waiter once gave me instructions on how his restaurant's buffet worked, which is the equivalent of my aunt taking Jeff Gordon aside to explain how to drive a standard shift.

ಬಂಡ

24 Arguing with stupidity is like mowing your lawn in a blizzard; a waste of time that wears you out while accomplishing nothing.

ಬಂಡ

25 It is a myth that your brain makes you who you are. In reality, your heart does.

26 *"It now seems that any statement made by anyone, once italicized, placed within quotation marks and posted online, is instantly elevated to a status of great insight and profundity, no matter how obvious or nonsensical it is."*-Chris Gay

༚༛

27 Since they don't make fake pigs, I wonder where imitation bacon bits come from.

༚༛

28 In life you have to learn to love yourself. Otherwise, you'll never make it as a narcissist.

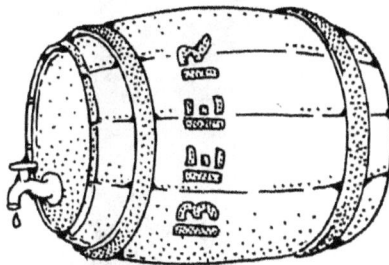

29 The one drawback to someone giving you a great birthday cake is that it always comes attached to having another birthday.

ဆၣႚ

30 If Benjamin Franklin were around today, I wonder how long it would take for his friends to tire of him using the line *"It's all about the me."*

ဆၣႚ

31 A mischievous ventriloquist could really mess with a mime's livelihood.

ဆၣႚ

32 Well clearly you're not illiterate.

33 I wish restaurants would stop leaving half of the pasta water in their chicken parmesan dish so I don't always need scuba gear to reach the cutlet.

ॐ

34 I had actually walked three full steps past a sign advertising *Extra-Large Bonsai Trees* before it hit me.

ॐ

35 Do you know what the difference is between a single man changing a burnt-out light bulb and one who is in a relationship? About three weeks.

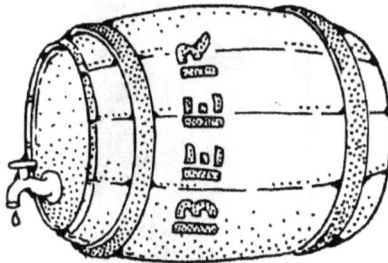

36 Can you imagine the impatience if we all suddenly had to revert back to using Polaroid cameras? *"60 seconds to develop?! What the hell am I supposed to do till then?!"*

൪൪

37 Actually, a watched pot will always boil. Unless the burner wasn't turned on high enough.

൪൪

38 In retrospect, I'm not sure that the fairly obvious advice *The Gambler* gave Kenny Rogers was worth the bottle of whiskey he gave up to hear it.

39 One thing you can always be sure of is that whenever someone starts a sentence with *"There's nothing worse than..."* there will be many, many things worse than whatever he or she completes that sentence with.

ഈര

40 Sometimes I ask myself where I see myself five years ago, and my answer always turns out to be exactly right.

ഈര

41 Ironically, it's okay to end a sentence with the word *preposition*.

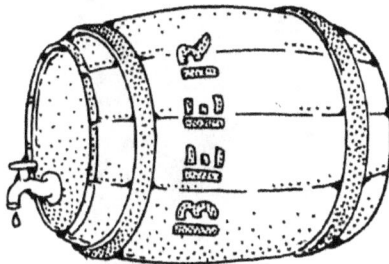

42 A true salad *bar* would include liquor so its patrons can console themselves for having to eat salad for dinner.

ಬಂಲ

43 Have you ever walked out of a store side-by-side with whoever else is leaving so that the endless parade of annoying fund-raisers outside will pitch them instead while you keep walking? No? Me neither. (Author's Note: This does not include Veterans, who deserve every penny they receive)

ಬಂಲ

44 Those birds seem more morose than angry.

45 Written on a bag of shredded cheddar cheese I'd bought was *Excellent Source of Calcium*. What's next, a sign in the Atlantic Ocean reading *Excellent Source of Salt Water*?

જી૭

46 I've never heard a carnivore say to his vegetarian host *"You know I can't eat that, there's lettuce in it."*

જી૭

47 Why doesn't someone invent an electric blanket with a *Cool* setting for hot nights? C'mon *General Electric*, do I have to think of everything?

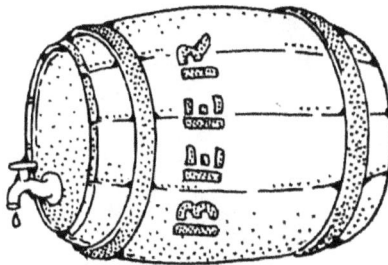

48 Real *Fantasy* Football would allow its owners to also draft cheerleaders from the professional teams that employ them.

❦

49 Darts and taverns have always seemed like an odd combination to me. *"Hey Bill, hold my beer while I throw this weighted needle across the room."*

❦

50 I've always found it somewhat amusing that the word *verb* is a noun.

51 It would be funny if there were separate tees for men and women on miniature golf courses, too.

ഇന്ദ്ര

52 Have you ever received a great offer only to feel less special after noticing that it was addressed to both you and *Current Resident*? They even capitalize the latter, as if he's some real guy listed in a phone book.

ഇന്ദ്ര

53 You often see churches decorated for Christmas, but never funeral homes decorated for Halloween.

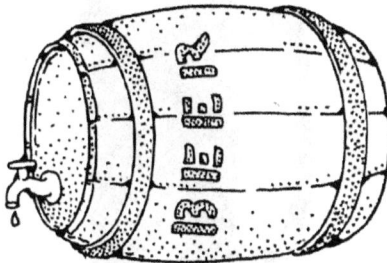

54 At what point do you think reality television show cameramen question their career choice?

৪০৫৪

55 It's ironic that banks once gave away toasters for opening accounts. You'd get their toaster, but they'd get your bread.

৪০৫৪

56 The irony, of course, is that there's no need to put forth any effort whatsoever to increase Breast Awareness.

57 Every network TV show seems to be set in New York, Chicago or San Francisco. Don't they have any hospitals, police stations or fire houses in Butte or Boise?

ဆဩ

58 I wish they didn't call those glasses *tumblers*. I don't appreciate companies that haven't even met me assuming I'm a klutz without at least giving me a chance to prove myself.

ဆဩ

59 Do you know what's tough to do when you're trying to fall asleep? Count sheep using Roman Numerals.

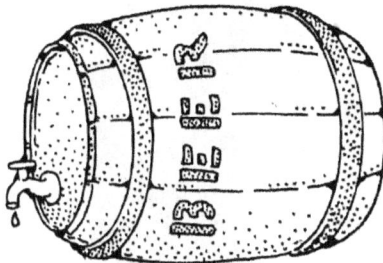

60 Belief without proof is more hope than faith.

ഇരുജ

61 Have you ever noticed that sometimes it takes hearing some group's cover version of a hit song years later for you to finally realize what the lyrics were?

ഇരുജ

62 People always seems to bet the devil their immortal souls. I'd never go that far; I'd just maybe ask if he'd accept some yard work in exchange for a pair of NHL season tickets.

ഇരുജ

63 I'm curious as to what part of the potato a *Pringle* comes from.

64   You almost never hear anyone say *"I don't want pizza tonight, let's get some British take-out food instead."*

ଓଓ

65   Authentic friends are the greatest wealth.

ଓଓ

66   One of my biggest disappointments after growing up was discovering that there was no meat already added to a can of *Sloppy Joe.*

ଓଓ

67   Thank God for those new-fangled knife sharpener infomercials. I can't tell you how many times I've unsuccessfully tried to slice a plum tomato with the dull edge of a credit card.

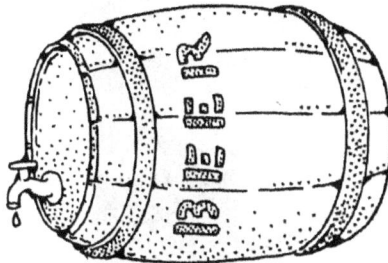

68 You can always count on me when the chips are up.

ೲೞ

69 I was surprised to discover Paul Sorvino had his own line of spaghetti sauce. At what point did the line distinguishing *character actor* and *celebrity* be redrawn so that the latter now includes people like this, and 80% of those who appear on *Celebrity Ghost Stories?*

ೲೞ

70 If my opinions were not correct, I'd have different ones.

71 To wish on a falling star seems like trying to benefit from the misfortune of others. I mean, if a carpenter fell off your roof it's unlikely you'd wish on him as he sailed past your window.

ಬಂಚ

72 Pet Peeve: When someone makes a point and then follows it up with *"In other words..."* before proceeding to make the same point again in simpler terms as if he thinks I'm *Forrest Gump.*

ಬಂಚ

73 When Stevie Wonder discovers something on his own that should have been obvious to whomever he's with, I wonder if he exclaims that even he could've seen that.

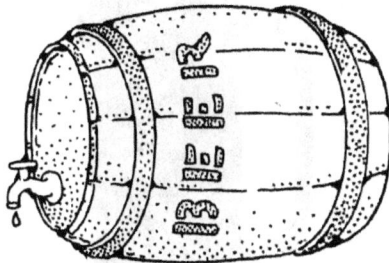

74 I'm curious as to how many monks choose that vocation merely because they're too shy to become mimes.

ಜೋಡ

75 They say there are no Atheists in foxholes; but they're probably not too many Agnostics in them, either.

ಜೋಡ

76 The duration of bad luck for mirror-breaking should be proportional based on size. A woman shouldn't get the same 7 years for dropping her compact as she might for cracking that thing Marlon Brando trapped General Zod with in *Superman*.

77 Whoever invents the first cost-effective outdoor air conditioner is going to become a multi-billionaire overnight.

ഗ്രരു

78 If the original *Jaws* were made today you can be certain that ten times as many Amity Island residents would be eaten, but that dog *Pippet* would survive.

ഗ്രരു

79 Just once I'd like to hear some honesty on a DVD commentary track. Does a film director really expect me to believe he considers himself lucky that Pauly Shore was available for the part?

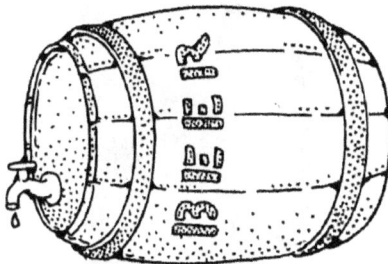

80 Have you ever noticed the difference in your mood when you wake up an hour before the time you'd set your alarm clock for, versus waking up three minutes before that same time?

ॐ

81 I wonder if British pedestrians in crosswalks are granted the left of way.

ॐ

82 I think I might be a psychic medium; whenever I walk into a liquor store I sense that I'm completely surrounded by spirits.

ॐ

83 If they ever invent a crayon eraser they should call it a *Crayoff.*

84 Did you ever notice how someone else's loud chewing is extremely annoying, yet yours doesn't bother you at all whatsoever?

೮೦೦೪

85 I wonder if a right-handed compliment would be one that's extra complimentary.

೮೦೦೪

86 A snare drum sounds more like an instrument that should capture a drumstick, rather than bounce it right back up to the drummer.

೮೦೦೪

87 The clocks built into those old-fashioned metal advertisements are really just a sign of the times.

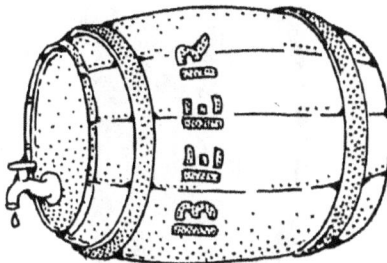

88 Whenever a sitcom ends with the words *"This episode was filmed before a live studio audience,"* I wonder what kind of audience the producer thinks viewers would otherwise expect. Not alive? Mannequins?

ଞଡଔଷ

89 In thanking toll-takers, I've for some reason just expressed gratitude to someone who's inconvenienced me, took my money and gave me nothing in return; the roads always suck anyway and there's not even a lousy moral lesson to be learned in the process.

ଞଡଔଷ

90 Do you know what's not very easy to do? Soak a colander.

91 You're never sure to live life as a sprint or marathon because you don't know where the finish line is. It's like trying to choose the right club for a hole of golf that you're going to play blindfolded.

೮ೞ

92 Dear Madison Avenue: I'm not trying to find the perfect Christmas gift for my spouse this year; I'm trying to find the perfect spouse this year for a Christmas gift.

೮ೞ

93 Upon exiting a highway I encountered a street sign reading *"Rough Road,"* and thought *"That's fairly profound, as life sure is."* As I drove on though I realized it was being literal. Damned grooved pavement.

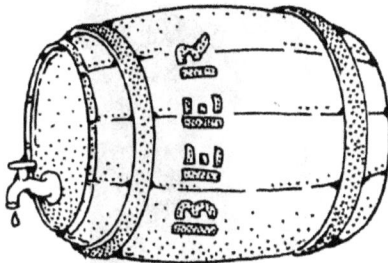

94 New England roadways in winter are fine; it's the ice and snow atop them that suck.

৪৫৪৪

95 Shouldn't peppercorn come on a cob?

৪৫৪৪

96 There should be a *Lukewarm Avenue* in every town so that no matter where you are, once you saw it, you'd always know that you were at least in the general area of your destination.

৪৫৪৪

97 I wonder why the 12-hour clock option the rest of us use isn't referred to as *Civilian Time*.

98 Some days I'm nostalgic for eras during which I wasn't even alive.

ഇൻഗ്ര

99 You know you're a New Englander when in the same October you're able to swim outdoors, yet also have to put a soda bottle left in the car overnight into the refrigerator so it can defrost.

ഇൻഗ്ര

100 I was never that good at table tennis. Whenever I took a step sideways I'd fall off.

ഇൻഗ്ര

101 It's hard to believe that the favorite treat of a city with as long and storied a history as San Francisco is a $1.99 box of flavored rice.

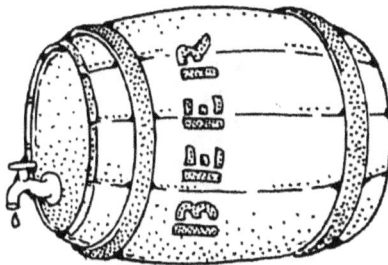

102 Sidekicks should have an out clause written into their contracts stating that, with proper notice, they can apply for open superhero jobs in other cities.

ℬℭ

103 I've never had a fear of heights; it's gravity that scares me.

ℬℭ

104 Both *time* and *thyme* rhyme with *rhyme*; though I don't think it really means anything.

ℬℭ

105 Creativity with words can be a pun thing.

106
This is not a Haiku
Go ahead count the syllables
I told you so

৪০৫৪

107
Why doesn't anyone ever use thin pretzel sticks in place of toothpicks when serving hors d'oeuvres?

৪০৫৪

108
It can't be said that those of us who are tall walk around with a bad altitude.

৪০৫৪

109
Though Agnostic, I'm still a firm believer in death after life.

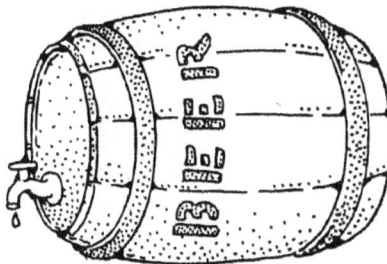

110 I wonder if anyone has ever ordered a can of Eggshell paint from a hardware store and got that milky brown color.

ഇരു

111 They should make miniature buns for cocktail franks.

ഇരു

112 Have you ever pushed your smartphone's *Check-In* button while home, and discovered a restaurant or shop listed that you had no idea was in your neighborhood?

113 If Jesus came back today, I couldn't even begin to fathom the fortune He'd amass in endorsement deals.

ಔಛ

114 The only time I'm ever judgmental of anyone is when I disagree with some aspect or another of his or her lifestyle.

ಔಛ

115 Why do women call those hairstyles *Permanents*? It really seems that they should be called *Temporaries*.

ಔಛ

116 I opened a fortune cookie to a fortune that read: *You're looking for luck in all the wrong places.*

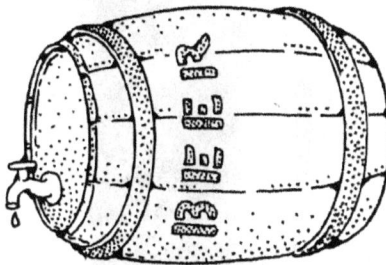

117 If you can't laugh at yourself, I'll do it for you.

୫୦ଓଃ

118 This works every time! Add your age to the year you graduated, then subtract 26. Multiply that number by 0, and the answer will always be 0!

୫୦ଓଃ

119 I'm curious as to what imitation vanilla extract is extracted from.

୫୦ଓଃ

120 Only a man could figure out how to get vodka out of a potato eleven hundred years before one of us gave any real thought to indoor plumbing.

121 I wonder how farmers tell if a cow has decided to give 1% or 2% milk that day.

☙ℭ☙

122 I'd really like to grow old with me.

☙ℭ☙

123 I can't imagine where our Founding Fathers found the time to sit around and think up all of those clever quotes that are constantly posted on social media.

☙ℭ☙

124 Some writers stick with fiction and humor simply to avoid writing those tedious, annoying footnotes. Or so I've heard.

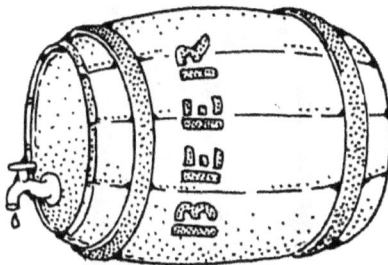

125 It must be tough for superheroes to launder their costumes. If Clark Kent won't even let Lois Lane know his identity, it's highly unlikely he'd divulge it to the counter guy at the Metropolis *Wash n' Wear*.

ಐಅ

126 You'd think that at least once in awhile you'd see a gingerbread condominium.

ಐಅ

127 What would you tell someone who's trying to ride a bike again after a long time without doing so? *"Don't worry, you can do it. It's just like, just like...Sorry, I got nothing."*

128 How about this for a great product idea? A waterproof bathroom strobe light for people who prefer to sing disco in the shower.

ಐಅಐ

129 Whether we recognize it or not, the music we grow up and older on is indeed the soundtrack of our lives.

ಐಅಐ

130 *"You don't say,"* said the passerby to the mime.

ಐಅಐ

131 If Doc Brown had found a lightning bug that produced 1.21 Gigawatts, Marty's trip back to 1985 would've been a much more interesting visual.

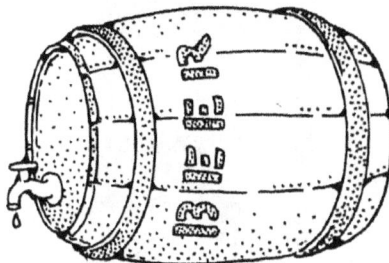

132 If Life hands you lemons, at least you're safe from Scurvy.

୫୦୯୫

133 Birthday clowns who specialize in making balloon dachshunds are just plain lazy.

୫୦୯୫

134 With great power comes great utility bills.

୫୦୯୫

135 If our Founding Fathers had declared Independence in January, I can't imagine how ridiculous the annual outdoor cookouts here in New England would look.

136 No matter the size of his financial wealth, a man without integrity is bankrupt.

৪৩৫৩

137 Have you ever made a can of chicken and dumplings just because you were craving the fried onions in your cupboard and needed something to put them on? No? Me neither.

৪৩৫৩

138 I wonder how long you're protected from vampires after eating a hot cross bun.

৪৩৫৩

139 I don't know why remembering passwords is so difficult for people; they all seem to be just a series of asterisks.

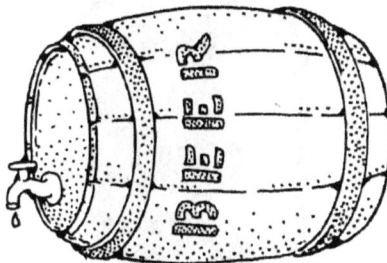

140 This year's Christmas tree was so difficult and exhausting to cut down that halfway through I considered converting to Judaism.

ༀ

141 I had planned to get my fortune told the other day, but as it turned out it just wasn't in the cards.

ༀ

142 When I go to a karaoke bar, I prefer to sing instrumentals.

ༀ

143 I was driving down Retreat Avenue in Hartford, Connecticut one day when, suddenly, I wasn't sure if I should keep going forward or turn around and go back.

144 Chris's Dictionary: *Intellectillusion.* (Noun) 1. The mistaken belief that your intelligence is greater than it actually is, simply because you saw one of your own thoughts showcased in a *Facebook* meme.

ಬಿಂ

145 I think it'd be much more fun to be de-motivational speaker.

ಬಿಂ

146 Eating a fortune cookie whole leads directly to a self-fulfilling prophecy.

ಬಿಂ

147 Time does indeed fly. I can remember the day preceding today as if it was only yesterday.

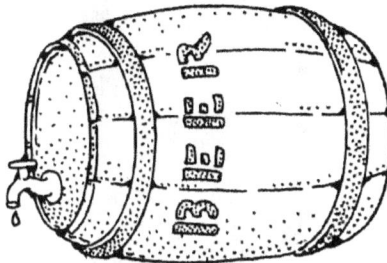

148 It's odd that chives get equal billing to sour cream. I doubt anyone's ever said, *"This potato would taste much better if only there were little tasteless flecks of green scattered atop it."*

⅋ᴑᴈ

149 If they made toy batteries, what would you use to run them?

⅋ᴑᴈ

150 Do cows called to the priesthood attend Bovinity School?

⅋ᴑᴈ

151 Politics and Religion should be like a buffet, not a set menu. Take what appeals to you, and leave behind that which you're not able or willing to swallow.

152 Does fake leather only pretend to shrink in the rain?

ଊଓଃ

153 If a brain surgeon and a rocket scientist are unable to complete a simple task together, I wonder if they pause a moment to give each other that knowing look of irony.

ଊଓଃ

154 Sometimes I look at a pizza flyer just to see what ridiculous new innovation they might've come up with lately, as at some point I fully expect to see cheese stuffed with cheese.

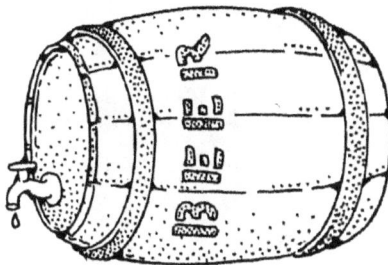

155 I walked by a Seafood Department tank with a sign on it reading *Fresh Caught Lobsters*. I'm glad they specified, as initially I'd thought that they had all just voluntarily surrendered.

&OCG

156 Some company actually makes an automatic, twirling spaghetti fork. What, no accompanying tabletop trebuchet to catapult the meatballs directly into your mouth?

&OCG

157 Whenever I walk through the middle of an empty parking lot and run into a spider's web, I always wonder where the hell it came from.

158 A funeral home would seem like the ideal place to have an attached bar.

ಬಌ

159 **PRESS HERE** for a special message on futility.

ಬಌ

160 When you come across the fine print on a jar of sauce, do you ever absent-mindedly try to enlarge the text by spreading your thumb and forefinger across it? No? Me neither.

ಬಌ

161 I wonder what French fry-flavored potato chips would taste like.

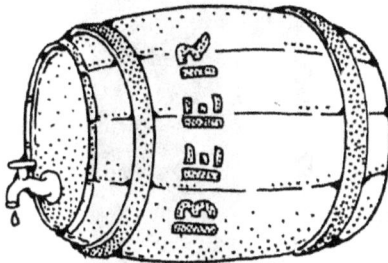

162 When I was very young I could never understand the point of a *"bottomless cup"* of coffee, as it seemed that any poured into it would just keep going straight through to the floor.

ଚଠ୫

163 One of the fringe benefits when you're between relationships is just covering up the pot of leftover pasta and tossing the whole thing into the refrigerator.

ଚଠ୫

164 I think it would be very tough to notice if an air guitar player switched to an air bass guitar.

165 It seems odd that canned preserves are stored in jars.

৪০৫৪

166 No matter how long it's been since I've seen it, my couch is always in the first place I look.

৪০৫৪

167 Of course what you see is what you get; it's what you hear that is at times misleading.

৪০৫৪

168 No matter how hard you try or how sloppy you write, it's impossible to forge your own signature.

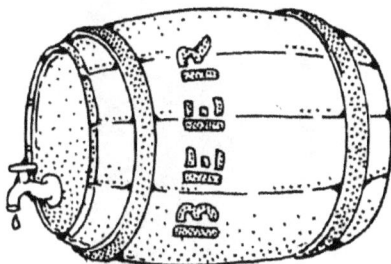

169 Would a feminist named *Mary Smith* who married a *John Smith* bother changing her name to *Mary Smith-Smith?*

ଧଔ

170 TV cooking show judges seem fairly pretentious. If I made Chicken Cacciatore out of fig leaves, walnut meat and cherry Pez in 30 minutes, only to hear some guy whose name only his wife knows tell me it might've been *"acceptable"* if I'd gone lighter on the orange zest, some serious sarcasm would ensue.

ଧଔ

171 *"I see what you're saying,"* said the man to the mime.

172 Memories make the best souvenirs...But I'm guessing you'll still buy that dumb stenciled coffee mug.

છાૈ

173 I'm not sure whether it's more frustrating to be an extroverted librarian or an introverted car salesman.

છાૈ

174 It seems like it took an awfully long time for people to realize that lighting Christmas trees with real candles was not such a great idea.

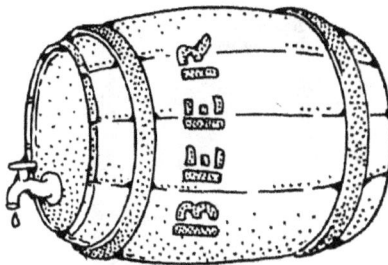

175 Have you ever put the radio on scan and come across the same song playing on two stations simultaneously, then for no reason kept toggling back and forth between them? No? Me neither.

ಬಂ಄

176 I can always count on an elevator to pick me up when I'm down.

ಬಂ಄

177 I hope hell does freeze over someday, just so that snowball would finally get its chance.

ಬಂ಄

178 *"You have too much time on your hands,"* said the man to the mover carrying a grandfather clock.

179 Instead of ticketing whoever caused an accident they should ticket its rubberneckers; especially when I'm running late.

ഇഐ

180 After watching a *Three Stooges* marathon, I can only conclude that OSHA didn't have nearly the same influence on the 1940's American workforce.

ഇഐ

181 It's kind of funny how long some people will circle the gym parking lot in an effort to snag the closest possible space to the door.

ഇഐ

182 For Lent this year I'm giving up religion.

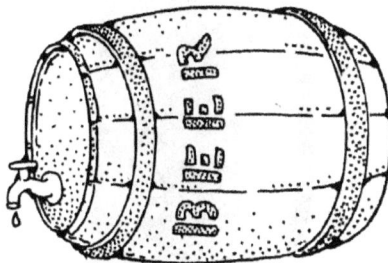

183 Re-enactment shows that change names to protect those whom the actors are portraying don't seem to mind the inconvenience they cause to the real people who actually have those fake names.

୫୦୯ଓ

184 Do you know what's tough to do? Tack a halo onto a snow angel.

୫୦୯ଓ

185 I'd love to live in the past because the rent was cheaper there.

186 Did I ever tell you guys about the time I started writing a wicked clever line, and then just trailed off in mid-senten

ಬಚಿ

187 Where do jugglers get their bowling pins? Buying an alley seems like a huge investment just to upgrade your act from oranges.

ಬಚಿ

188 Have you ever laid down on your couch to watch hockey with a cat around? They're like mini-Great White sharks. For twenty seconds a tail circles the ottoman, then it's gone. Three minutes later, right in front of you from out of nowhere pops up a furry little face bellowing a ferocious meow.

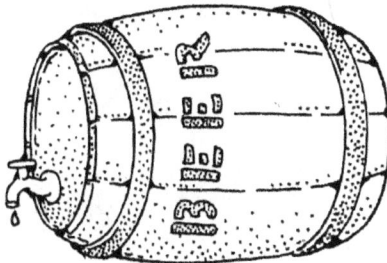

189 Though I'm not particularly religious, I do watch those *History Channel* Bible specials just in case there are any new…Revelations.

ဆဟ

190 A smartphone battery light is like your car's gas light. When either goes on, you immediately start to calculate just how long you can last without making an effort to rectify the situation.

ဆဟ

191 I think *Manna from Heaven* would make a great name for a national bread company.

192 For a little turnabout, it'd be cool if *Mrs. Smith's* would make a pumpkin pie that comes in a Plain Wax Candle scent.

⊰⊱

193 I wonder if crabs are more offended or relieved by imitation crabmeat.

⊰⊱

194 We really should consider applying across-the-board minimum intellect requirements.

⊰⊱

195 What if historians meant to write 'The *Holey* Grail,' and it turns out that all this time we should've been looking for a colander?

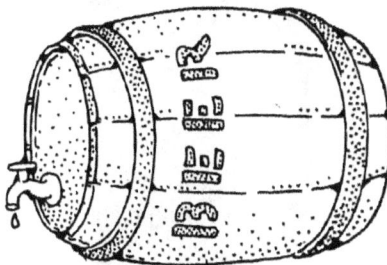

196 All I can say about these desktop oscillating, air-redistribution devices is, I'm a fan.

ဆလ

197 People will say anything to make themselves feel better. Have you ever heard a 25-year old say *"Age is just a number. You're only as old as you feel"*?

ဆလ

198 Let he who is without aim cast the first stone at me.

199 You'd think that a mosquito would avoid a bug zapper by using the same logic humans do when we elect not to send manned space flights to the sun.

ഓദ

200 You can't live and learn if you don't try to learn from living.

ഓദ

201 Some days I think myself a maverick; a throwback to a simpler time when men were men. Then I remember I still use the chart printed inside the chocolate box cover to ensure that I don't get a nougat one.

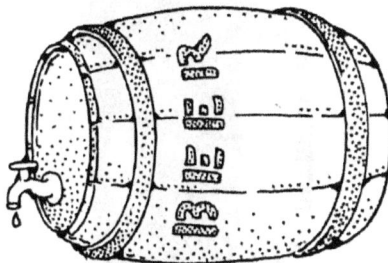

202 Have you ever noticed that the owl's eyes in the Hooters' restaurant logo look exactly like a gigantic pair of…Oh, wait. Hold on. I think that's my phone.

ഈരു

203 At some point in the 1960's there was a TV theme song lyricist who began collecting royalties for writing the word *Batman* twenty-nine times in a 60-second spot.

ഈരു

204 Do mischievous coal miners receive candy in their Christmas stockings?

ഈരു

205 I've always had strength enough to make it through yesterday.

206 There must be thousands of Generation X'ers who own the *A* volume of the *Funk & Wagnalls'* encyclopedia set that sold for $.09 in grocery stores. Each succeeding volume cost $10 apiece though, which is why we know what an aardvark is but can't tell you much about the Bastille.

ೞೞೞ

207 You only get one chance to make a 3rd impression.

ೞೞೞ

208 If they debuted a show called *American Grammar*, it's doubtful that there would be enough contestants left for a second episode.

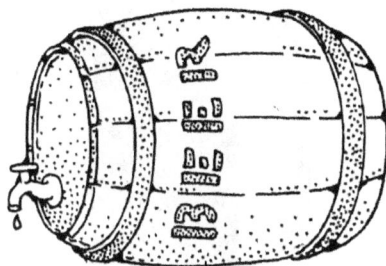

209 I wonder if the ancient Romans used our system of numbers when they wanted to make one of their sporting events sound impressive.

ഇരുന്ന

210 None of my get rich slow schemes seem to be working, either.

ഇരുന്ന

211 The book review I like least is *"It was a page-turning read..."* Every single book ever written is a page-turning read. It's like reviewing a Domino's and calling their product *"An edible, sliced pizza."*

212 It'd be cool if one of those television mediums could somehow contact the *Ghost of Common Sense* and, if so, beg it to reincarnate.

හැ⊙ශ

213 Rather than adversity, it would be great if significant contentment or utter nirvana could build character once in a while.

හැ⊙ශ

214 I like to be very specific about my generalizations.

හැ⊙ශ

215 Sure, those invisible cars sound cool, but invisible junk food would be more helpful.

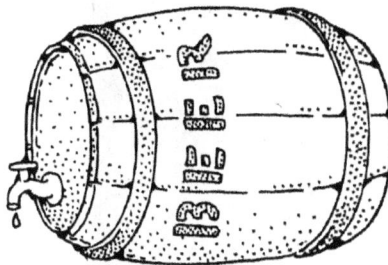

216 I think it'd be funny if you gave someone a ball of string and said *"Unfortunately, this gift does come with some strings attached."*

80C3

217 It seems that the most important factor in creating a successful microbrew beer is to come up with as dumb a name as possible.

80C3

218 I think it would be cool if people actually said *"expletive!"* in place of whatever obscenity they were going to use.

80C3

219 Why doesn't a deer ever seem to jump out in front of a car when it's stopped at a red light?

220 Crickets must get very tired of their family and friends chirping at them all the time.

஘௸

221 B Baker Street. See what I did there?

஘௸

222 You show me a millionaire who'd try and start a ferry service across a brook, and I'll show you a bored eccentric with a great sense of humor.

஘௸

223 There should be a more reasonable list of transgressions that if broken would still get us into Heaven, such as '*The 7 Somewhat Frowned-Upon Sins.*' I mean you never hear stuff like "*An extra serving of bacon go-eth before the fall.*"

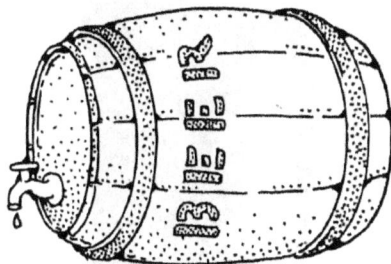

224 Do they really need to make both Angel Hair pasta and thin spaghetti?

৵ল

225 It strikes me as odd that no group ever seems to put a watch in their time capsule.

৵ল

226 Have you ever wondered what would happen if you left an Angel Food cake and a Devil's Food cake on the same counter, and then left the room?

227 One overlooked benefit to New Year's Day is that you are instantly certain of another year that won't appear on the right side of your tombstone.

ဧ၀ဗ

228 I think it would be funny to hear James Earl Jones say: *"I know you are, but what am I?"*

ဧ၀ဗ

229 I'd imagine police get fairly annoyed during the normal course of their workday due to every person they get behind driving no more than 25 miles per hour.

ဧ၀ဗ

230 You'd have to be a world class stuntman to pop a wheelie on a unicycle.

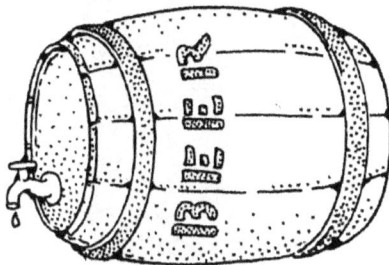

231 The world would be a much better place if I determined who was allowed to renew their driver's license and whose would be indefinitely suspended. Well better for me, at least.

ଔଔ

232 I once tried to watch a show about how breakfast cereal is made, but the footage was too grainy.

ଔଔ

233 Contrary to popular belief a writer's best friends are not caffeine and music; they're synonyms.

234 In the 1800's people answered a telephone with *"Ahoy."* That would sound much cooler today, especially if you're in a bad mood. *"Ahoy! No damn it, I don't have Prince Albert in a can!"*

₧₨

235 Recently as I considered taking the highway or a more scenic route, the radio played *Supertramp's Take the Long Way Home.* I took the highway, just in case Karma was trying to screw with me.

₧₨

236 Why do so many spirit mediums cleanse houses with salt? Would a demon emerge from hell, look down, and actually say *"Wait, is that salt? I can't cross a seasoning. Damn it, I'll be the laughing stock of the 9th Circle."*

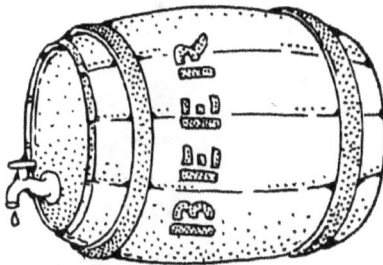

237 That's the thing about Italian food. You have some, and then three days later you're hungry again.

∽∾

238 This year I took full advantage of the *Black Friday* and *Cyber Monday* sales. I didn't buy a single thing on either and it's true; I saved a fortune.

∽∾

239 It astounds me that Minnesota has exactly 10,000 lakes.

∽∾

240 If political ignorance were hairspray, there'd be nothing left of the Ozone Layer.

241 It's amazing that you can make wine, grape juice, and raisins from the same little fruit. Let's see a zucchini do that.

ഔഗ

242 Caterers gonna cate.

ഔഗ

243 Under different circumstances, re-arranging the deck chairs on the *Titanic* might very well have been a sound aesthetic choice.

ഔഗ

244 Waiting for what your heart wants does not make you shallow.

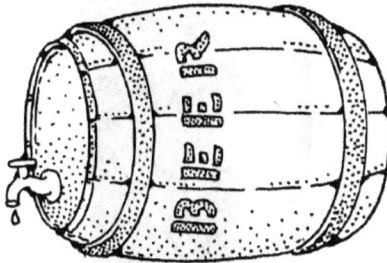

245 As I was buying vodka once I remembered that it's a good thing to drink a lot of water, too. So I added a bag of ice.

ଽଓଓଷ

246 Volume does not equal substance.

ଽଓଓଷ

247 I'm curious as to how many accidents occur while a driver is staring into his rearview mirror to see if the cop he just passed is pulling out of his speed trap.

248 Sometimes I watch *The Newlywed Game* and wonder where the questions like *"Did you settle?"* are. Hey, those contestants are playing for big money. They should earn it.

ಬಂಣ

249 Shipping magnates always seem to be billionaires; you never hear about any middle class shipping magnates.

ಬಂಣ

250 If a wishing well runs dry, just toss in a quarter and ask for more water.

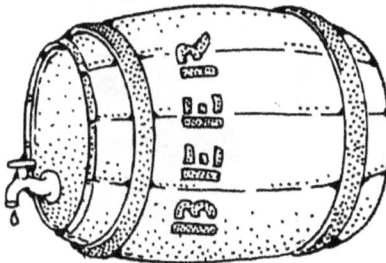

251 Do you know why you brush your teeth longest with a new toothbrush? Because your subconscious understands it's the cleanest that brush will ever be.

ಐಂಲ

252 Since baseball has *C, D, AA* and *AAA* leagues, it stands to reason that they should have a *9 Volt* league as well.

ಐಂಲ

253 In hindsight, I wonder if Noah wishes he would have left those two politicians off of the Arc.

254 Pet Peeve: Radio DJ's who still think it's 1983 and awkwardly stretch out their prattling over the start of a great song in an obvious attempt to hit the post.

ಬಂಡ

255 Sometimes I'll hang up a take-out menu I'd never order from just to showcase a cool refrigerator magnet.

ಬಂಡ

256 To refrain from drinking is a truly sobering experience.

ಬಂಡ

257 I think you could at least succeed at some of your goals by only pulling out a couple of the stops.

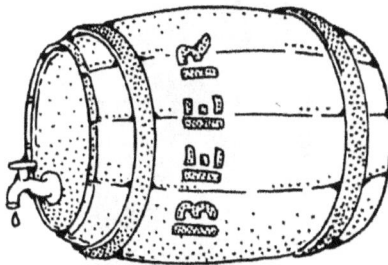

258 While *accept* and *except* sound alike, if you sent an invitation reading *"I'm having a party for all of my friends, and nothing would give me greater pleasure than to except your RSVP"* you'd come across as a cold bastard, because *except* means *to exclude*. Grammar counts.

෩෮

259 At least eggs are always all that they're cracked up to be.

෩෮

260 The only thing I can come up with is that in some previous life I must have gotten every conceivable break.

261 Do you know what would be a practical investment? Social Life Insurance. That way if you turned out to be an introvert you could at least live comfortably.

୫୬୯ଓ

262 I wonder if Andrew Ridgeley and DJ Jazzy Jeff get together for coffee once in a while just to commiserate on what might have been.

୫୬୯ଓ

263 They should make disposable dress shirts for people who really don't like to iron.

୫୬୯ଓ

264 Some say that *"if animals could talk, we'd all be vegetarians."* However if plants could talk we'd all be carnivores. So it evens out.

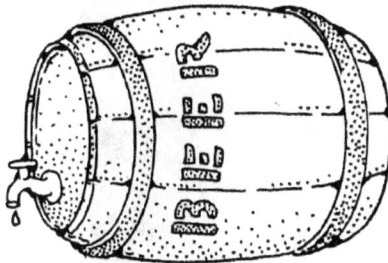

265 A tub of margarine I bought had *"Tastes Like Real Butter"* printed on it, but truth be told I don't know what fake butter tastes like, anyway.

ᏪᎤᏟᎦ

266 No matter what's written on the box, there's no such thing as a *"hint"* of anything in sugar cereal.

ᏪᎤᏟᎦ

267 Only a real dummy would hang out with a ventriloquist.

ᏪᎤᏟᎦ

268 As it turns out, the definition of *"Hater"* is actually not *"Anyone with opinions that differ from yours."*

269 Shouldn't a food's shelf-life depend primarily on the sturdiness of the shelf?

ജ

270 While studying for something, you can read the same material for weeks and not retain any of it; but hear an annoying song for one second and you can't forget it for days.

ജ

271 It's interesting that a note home from an illiterate Civil War soldier might read: *"My Dearest Love, I beseech thee to maintain thy inner strength, for on my life and sacred honor, no man nor conflict could ever forestall my safe return to you. With great affection…"* Yet today we get: *"CU l8r, Bee-yotch. U lookd HOT this a.m. Can't w8 4 a piece o that love muffin."*

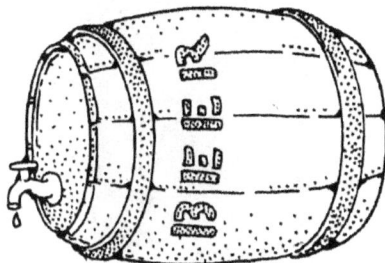

272 Why are the ancient sayings of Confucius all in English?

೫೦೦೩

273 Nothing brings you back to the 1970's faster than an uncharged cell phone during a power outage. All that's missing are avocado green and mustard yellow kitchen appliances.

೫೦೦೩

274 Yes, Virginia. Well, kind of. What there really is, is a significant corporate presence heavily counting on your belief in Santa Claus.

275 There has to be at least a couple of dumb-Alec's out there. In fact I'm almost sure I've seen some on TV.

ഇൻ

276 If you produced a line of men's shampoo costing $0.75 a bottle, you'd probably corner the market.

ഇൻ

277 Why is it that in the time it takes you to walk from your couch to your bed you go from half asleep to wide awake?

ഇൻ

278 How much time would you imagine a cat spends thinking about the Tax Code? We're the only creatures who make things harder on ourselves than they have to be.

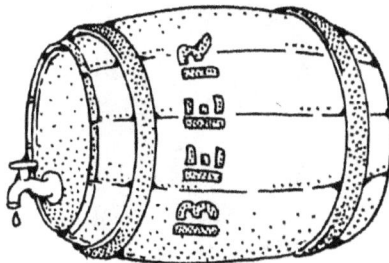

279 I think that most people would actually prefer to avoid finding a needle in a haystack. Especially by surprise.

ഇരുൻ

280 Did you ever wonder whether *Hobbes* was a real tiger and *Calvin* was his imaginary friend who only came to life when other tigers weren't around? If you haven't, you are now.

ഇരുൻ

281 The other day I drove a half-marathon and felt fantastic!

282 While watching a pre-1990's movie, does it ever occur to you how hugely different the plot or outcome would be for many of them if only some of the characters could have had access to a lousy cell phone?

ഗ്രജ

283 Have you ever noticed how friends of yours are your *buddies* or *pals*, while friends of people you don't like are their *cronies?*

ഗ്രജ

284 Whenever someone tells you of an experience that *"scared them to death,"* the only part of their story that you can believe with certainty is that it didn't.

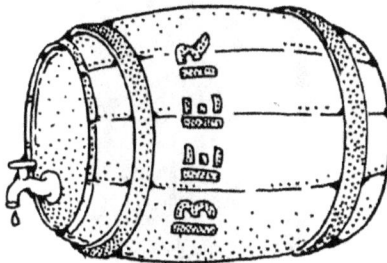

285 Clearing out the snow clogging up the space between my wheel and fender provides a satisfaction similar to that of finally getting a thread of corn silk unstuck from between two back teeth.

৪০৫৪

286 The Meek won't inherit the Earth. The Ignorant will.

৪০৫৪

287 I can't imagine how tough it must be for a vampire to remain inconspicuous in a hair salon. (This is a mirror joke)

288 If you trademarked the 'blur' that TV uses to cover t-shirt logos they're not authorized to show, would they then have to create a fake product logo to cover your trademarked 'blur'?

ഇ൯ദ

289 Even if your piece of toast actually landed on the floor butter-side up, I'm guessing you wouldn't really want to eat it anyway.

ഇ൯ദ

290 A sheep in wolf's clothing could really have a lot of fun at the expense of other sheep.

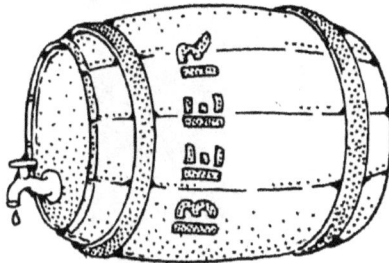

291 At some point in the 1970's, some guy was hooking up a telephone answering machine while listening to his 8 Track cassettes and thinking to himself "Really, this has just got to be as far as technology can go."

ೞଓ

292 Have you ever bought your wife or girlfriend something by phone from *Frederick's of Hollywood* instead of going into the store, just so they'd send you their catalogue of hot models for the next decade? No? Me neither.

ೞଓ

293 How do you tell when croutons have gone stale?

294 In the movies, no good ever seems to come to anyone living on or near a house built over an old Indian burial ground.

ಜೌಞ

295 It's cool when you wake up and see that the time on the digital clock shows your birthday. However if you were born in December and this happens often, you're probably kind of lazy. But I digress.

ಜೌಞ

296 It is somewhat surprising that there's not a *'Caution: May turn slippery after contact with water'* warning label on bath soap by now.

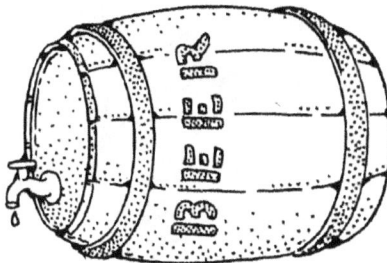

297 I wonder if *The Grinch* ever got tired of some random dude inexplicably setting his most nefarious character traits to music, and then following him around all day singing them to anyone within earshot.

೮೦೮೪

298 Those football fans who wear a block of Styrofoam cheese on their heads look like they're playing the world's largest game of *Trivial Pursuit,* and all they can answer is the *History* question.

೮೦೮೪

299 If you didn't have butterflies, you probably settled.

300 I can't figure out why there's a *mute* button on my car radio. The *off* button is six inches closer and with less effort accomplishes the same result.

ഇരുൽ

301 Did Charles Dickens really expect us to believe that *Ebenezer Scrooge's* life-changing conversion was permanent, when most of us can't even keep one New Year's Resolution past January 3rd?

ഇരുൽ

302 Actually, what I could really use is a self-cleaning *toaster* oven.

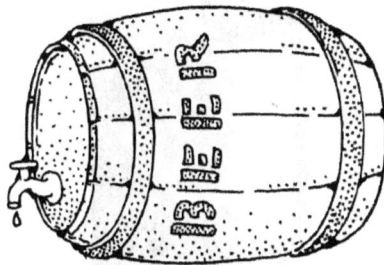

303 Only astronauts can truly understand the gravity of their situation.

ଔଔଔ

304 You never seem to see anyone *Check-in* on a smartphone from a proctologist's office.

ଔଔଔ

305 An attractive woman who covers herself with tattoos is like Leonardo da Vinci opting to spray-paint a dessert course onto *The Last Supper.*

ଔଔଔ

306 I don't do *'Holiday'* parties. What if you get there and it turns out that they're celebrating a boring one like Arbor Day?

307 You'd probably have to begrudgingly respect the first state to drop the pretense and just sew a '$' on its flag.

୫୦୦ଓ

308 It must suck living on the time zone lines and having to always triple check tee times, movie times, and etcetera. Or worse, you go over to your neighbor's house for an hour and end up returning home before you'd even left.

୫୦୦ଓ

309 If Mother Nature had wanted us to clean up kitchen spills, she never would have invented evaporation.

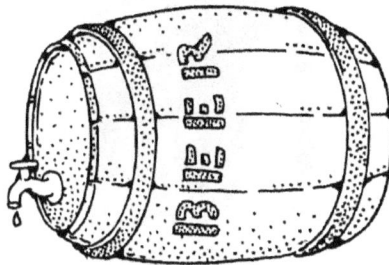

310 We mine coal to burn and we drill oil to burn. So where the hell does all of that scented candle wax come from?

ಶಿಂ

311 If I ever came across a message in a bottle that read *Please don't litter*, at least I'd know that somewhere in the world someone else has my sense of humor.

ಶಿಂ

312 If food scientists can make *Doritos* taste like chili or cheeseburgers, they should be able to make broccoli taste like bacon.

313 It's odd that James Bond's every mission is to some exotic locale or another. You would think that MI6 would have to send him somewhere like Detroit once in a while.

୫୦୯୪

314 I have an idea for a movie script in which four gorgeous women form a ghost-hunting team near a California beach and investigate haunted mud volleyball courts, Jacuzzis, and pillow fights. The twist is that whether they find ghosts or not, they're all still really, really hot.

୫୦୯୪

315 If you don't fall in love with a dreamer, there'd be no one left.

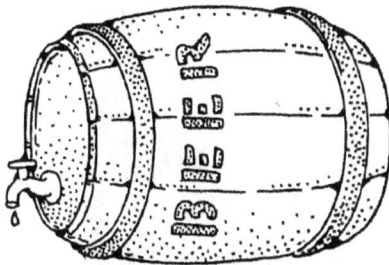

316 You can effectively teach integrity only to those who want to be taught.

ଔଔ

317 Products that boast of containing 10% real juice, cheese, and etcetera, never seem to boast at all about what makes up the other 90%.

ଔଔ

318 You'd think that by now someone, maybe under the brand name *Ring Tea-ones*, would have invented tea kettles that can whistle custom songs for you.

319 Sometimes, everything that you've ever wanted is right in front of you. And sometimes, you have to go back to the fridge for the catsup.

ဆဂဒ

320 You may have noticed that when some people speak of *tolerance*, what they mean is they want tolerance of their views; not of yours.

ဆဂဒ

321 A dollar store was selling pregnancy test kits, and I was relieved to discover that an instrument I might rely on to disclose to me the biggest news of my life can be purchased for the same price as a box of *Sno-Caps*.

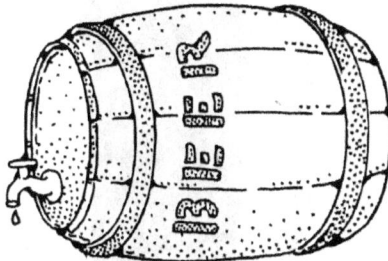

322 I'm so happy to have me in my life.

ဆၢ

323 As there seems to be a mainstream horror movie based on every holiday except Thanksgiving, how about this: The vengeful spirit of William Bradford possesses a world champion turkey carver, who then becomes *The Pilgrim*, a menacing...Okay, yeah. Maybe I should consider switching to decaf diet soda.

ဆၢ

324 We could use tip calculators that factor in poor service.

325 The two major impacts of erosion we seem unable to stop are that of the Niagara River on its Falls, and what was once an actual half gallon container of ice cream.

ଞ୦ଔ

326 If all the cows came home one day, would all of the yelling and complaining worldwide come to a sudden stop?

ଞ୦ଔ

327 Do you think *Wonder Woman* really has to expend much effort tying guys up with her magic lasso, or do you think most of them just kind of go with it voluntarily?

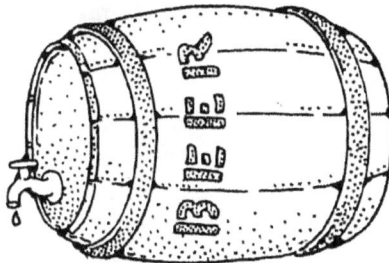

328 You see a lot of *buddy-cop* movies, but not too many featuring *buddy-optometrists*.

ಬೃಙ

329 If extreme cold numbs pain, why do those ice cream headaches hurt so damn much?

ಬೃಙ

330 It seems clear that in 1971 Alan Shepard didn't really consider the possibility of an *eBay* when he decided to leave the golf balls he hit on the moon…on the moon.

ಬೃಙ

331 Why is canned, dehydrated milk wet?

332 I've decided not to spend any time at all worrying about Y3K; I'll just deal with it when it gets here.

ഓരു

333 The irony of a broken vacuum cleaner is that it sucks...because it doesn't suck.

ഓരു

334 Dramas like *24* should have Christmas episodes like sitcoms do. Maybe decorate CTU with stockings and, after Jack Bauer beats information out of a suspect, they can drink eggnog while other agents gather 'round to sing carols.

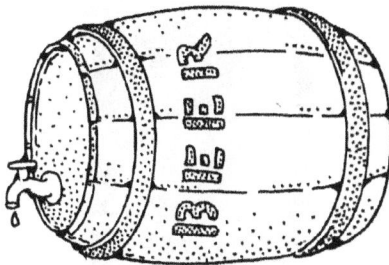

335 The fax machine was invented in 1843. I'm fairly certain you think that was either a typo or a joke and will verify. Once you do, I predict you'll toss that little tidbit out at parties for years to come without ever giving either me or this book credit for letting you know. It's okay though, I understand.

ജ◌ൽ

336 If a stage actor actually does break a leg during a performance, I wonder if you're then etiquette-bound to revert back to wishing him or her *Good luck* in future shows.

ജ◌ൽ

337 For some seafood restaurants, it's all about sole.

338 I can't be the only one who thinks that snorkels should be much longer.

ಬಿಂಜ

339 The other day I actually craved a fresh green salad. Perhaps I've-wait for it-turned over a new leaf.

ಬಿಂಜ

340 I wouldn't be a bit surprised to learn that the delegates to the *Continental Congress* decided to meet in Philadelphia solely for those delicious cheesesteaks.

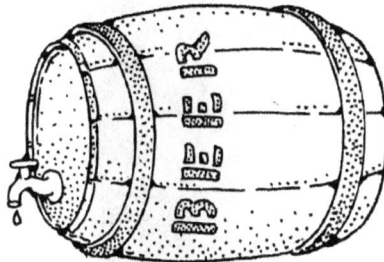

341 Whenever someone prefaces a statement with *"With all due respect..."* it's nearly always followed by something disrespectful.

ಐ©ಐ

342 From the first moment I met oxygen, I knew from that day on we'd never be apart for as long as I lived.

ಐ©ಐ

343 Somewhere there has got to be a huge pile of those plastic yellow discs that we snapped into 45 RPM records so they'd play on our 33 RPM turntables. Surely they could be reused as...I got nothing.

344 To the dental receptionists who schedule my next appointment nine months in the future and then ask me whether 10a.m. or 10:15a.m. is better: Really?

ଚ୍ଚେ

345 A proud writer stores his books on his bookshelf. A narcissistic writer, in his bathroom.

ଚ୍ଚେ

346 *Swear* should really be considered a swear word. I mean, it's kind of *the* swear word.

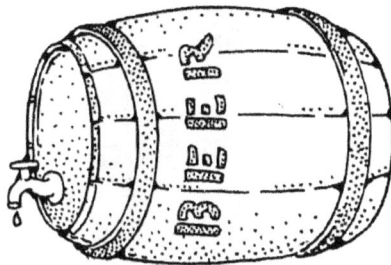

347 Every winter I thank Heaven for the New England weathermen who constantly remind me that, should I need to go out into a raging blizzard, to *"drive carefully."* Thanks for the sage advice, but this ain't my first rodeo.

ಬಿಂ

348 I wonder if the politically correct persons who are trying to extinguish the word *Christmas* realize that their preferred replacement, *Holiday*, is a derivative of the term *Holy Day*. Perhaps the lesson here is that the faux self-righteous should take an Etymology class.

349 I don't understand guys who consume ghost chili peppers; life is tough enough without ordering food that won't be served to you without your first having signed a waiver.

ෂංෆ

350 The manufacturers of invisible tape don't appear to realize that stuff you can see is not invisible.

ෂංෆ

351 It would be fantastic if some company somewhere is currently building a flush kitchen wastebasket.

ෂංෆ

352 It's kind of funny that salt is used both to make ice cream and to melt ice.

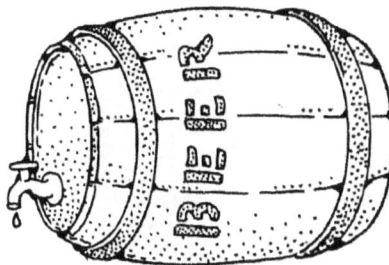

353 I wonder if anyone who owns one would see the humor in hiding a wall safe behind the portrait of a wall safe.

ଧଠଓ

354 I wish all of the Jennifers I know would collectively agree to nickname themselves either *Jen* or *Jenn*. It'd be nice if just once those selfish ladies would think about accuracy-preoccupied writers for a change.

ଧଠଓ

355 In a world without sarcasm, there wouldn't be any.

356 I like olive oil but I don't understand how anything can be *"extra virgin."* It either is or it isn't, with no embellishment required.

ഇരുള

357 You'd think that at least once in a while one of those little tour boats would become stranded on a charted, inhabited isle.

ഇരുള

358 When you leave the light on to read in bed and then get comfortable, it's funny how suddenly *The Clapper* no longer seems like the asinine idea it did when you first saw the commercial.

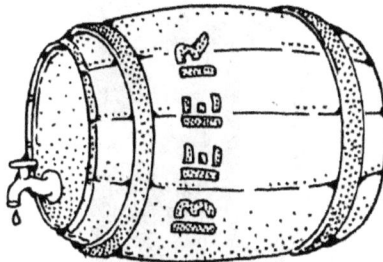

359 I'm not sure why vertical counter-top paper towel holders have a screw-on knob up top. Is the manufacturer really concerned that without it the towels might try to make a break for it once everyone leaves the kitchen?

ಬಂಡ

360 Although British singers lose their accents when they perform, those of country singers seem to somehow become enhanced.

ಬಂಡ

361 Just because you *can* talk doesn't mean it's a requirement.

362 Lots of people say *"You never know..."* But most of the time if you wait long enough you'll find out.

ဆာ

363 I find it mildly ironic that an officials' *safe* call in baseball is identical to an officials' *out* call in boxing; though not ironic enough to care all that much.

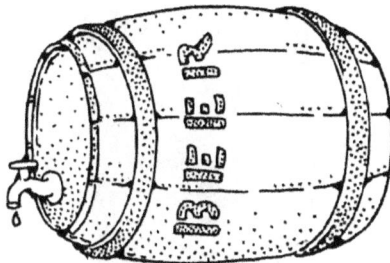

364

For the betterment of all mankind, please keep this key handy whenever you decide to post anything online. Thank you!

There = Location.
Their = Possession.
They're = Contraction. (They are)

Your = Possession.
You're = Contraction. (You are)

To = Direction.
Too = Also, very.
Two = Number. (Follows one, precedes three)

Looser = Less tight.
Loser = One who doesn't know the difference between the two by now.

365

What can:

Bring joy, sorrow, laughter or comfort?

Persuade or dissuade?

Indicate great intellect or monumental stupidity?

Enflame or diffuse a situation?

Create powerful memories, patriotism, or a compulsion to help others?

Elicit great emotion?

Stay with you forever?

The answer? Words. Please try to use them wisely, as almost nothing else that you have control over will ever have the power to make as great an impact on others.

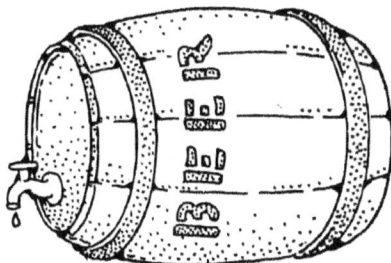

Afterword

The thing is, a book like this doesn't really need an Afterword. However the original had one so this one probably should, too. Besides, this is a great way to get in one more shameless plug for my additional writings. (And that's not even including the *About the Author* blurb to follow) So if you've enjoyed what you've just read, why not give my other books a try? There are the hysterical *The Bachelor Cookbook: Edible Meals with a Side of Sarcasm*, *Something Witty this Way Comes* and *And That's the Way it was…Give or Take: A Daily Dose of My Radio Writings*, or even *Shouldn't Ice Cold Beer be Frozen? My 365 Random Thoughts to Improve Your Life Not One Iota*. Perhaps you're looking for some substantive literature. If so, there's my paranormal, theological thriller novel *Ghost of a Chance*. In it, God and the devil begin the story with a pancake shop bet during the 1993 blizzard in Hartford. Or try *Sherlock Holmes and the Final Reveal*; an original novella I wrote in the classic style, with the most incredible twist ever written in a Holmes story. I'm also writing the Ghost of a Chance sequel *Perdition's Wrath,* and the Christmas tale *Kringle: From Man to Myth*. Whatever it is that you like to read, I've probably got the book for you. Surely you've got a search engine around somewhere, so check them out online and get yourself a copy or two. Or more. Yeah, more sounds good. All right, that's it. So…good-bye.

About the Author

Chris Gay is an author, freelance writer, voice-over artist, broadcaster and actor. He writes and broadcasts a daily, minute radio humor spot in Hartford, Connecticut. He's also written the paranormal, theological thriller novel *Ghost of a Chance*, the novella *Sherlock Holmes and the Final Reveal* and four other humor books: *The Bachelor Cookbook: Edible Meals with a Side of Sarcasm, Shouldn't Ice Cold Beer Be Frozen? My 365 Random Thoughts to Improve Your Life Not One Iota, And That's the Way It Was...Give or Take: A Daily Dose of My Radio Writings*, and *Something Witty This Way Comes*. He's been published nationally in *Writer's Digest* and is currently writing the Ghost of a Chance sequel *Perdition's Wrath* and a Christmas story *Kringle: From Man to Myth*. Chris has written and voiced radio commercials, authored both comedic and non-comedic freelance articles, scripts, press releases, website, media and technical content, done occasional radio color commentary for local sports, and acted in a couple of movies and plays. His website is chrisjgay.com, and his humor blog can be found at chrisgay.wordpress.com.

Still thirsty to read more? Check out my website and blog, whose addresses are conveniently listed below. In fact, here they are now:

My website: www.chrisjgay.com
My Blog: chrisgay.wordpress.com

www.chrisjgay.com

www.ingramcontent.com/pod-product-compliance
Lightning Source LLC
Chambersburg PA
CBHW071132090426
42736CB00012B/2099